The House That Love Built

By
Annie J. Adams, Ph.D.

Published by
Queen V Publishing
Englewood, OH
QueenVPublishing.com

Queen V Publishing
Englewood, OH
QueenVPublishing.com
Copyright © 2024 by Annie J. Adams, Ph.D.

All rights reserved. No part of this book may be reproduced or transmitted in any form or by any means, electronic or mechanical, without prior written consent of the author, except for the inclusion of brief quotes in a review.
Library of Congress Control Number: 2024911880
ISBN-13: 978-1-7358162-4-1
Cover design and illustrations by Sona and Jacob
Edited by Valerie J. Lewis Coleman of Pen of the Writer and Keitorria Edmonds of the Final Edit Co

Printed in the United States

These are the doors that open wide,
as we go inside the house that love built.

These are the windows that meet the sun, where the doors open wide, as we go inside the house that love built.

These are the greeters who lead the way, past the windows that meet the sun, where the doors open wide, as we go inside the house that love built.

These are the pews, fixed to the floor, that seat the people led by greeters, past the windows that meet the sun, where the doors open wide, as we go inside the house that love built.

This is the altar where we kneel to pray, while the piano plays songs of praise and our voices raise, beyond the pews fixed to the floor, that seat the people led by greeters, past the windows that meet the sun, where the doors open wide, as we go inside the house that love built.

This is the cross of Him who died for us all, that hangs above the altar where we kneel to pray, while the piano plays songs of praise and our voices raise, beyond the pews fixed to the floor, that seat the people led by greeters, past the windows that meet the sun, where the doors open wide, as we go inside the house that love built.

This is the Book of Love about Him who died for us all, above the altar where we kneel to pray, while the piano plays songs of praise and our voices raise, beyond the pews fixed to the floor, that seat the people led by greeters, past the windows that meet the sun, where the doors open wide, as we go inside the house that love built.

What is the little boy doing in each bubble?

Granny Annie is available to speak to your children about Christian living and character building. Connect with her at DrAnnieJAdams.com.

For bulk purchases, the companion coloring book, and more activities, visit TheHouseThatLoveBuilt.net or scan the QR code.

Answers: praying (red), praising (yellow), singing (green)

www.ingramcontent.com/pod-product-compliance
Lightning Source LLC
Chambersburg PA
CBHW041526070526
44585CB00002B/102